HOORAY FOR FIREFIGHTERS!

by Tessa Kenan

BUMBA BOOKS™

LERNER PUBLICATIONS ◆ MINNEAPOLIS

Note to Educators:

Throughout this book, you'll find critical thinking questions. These can be used to engage young readers in thinking critically about the topic and in using the text and photos to do so.

Lerner Publications Company
A division of Lerner Publishing Group, Inc.
241 First Avenue North
Minneapolis, MN 55401 USA

For reading levels and more information, look up this title at www.lernerbooks.com.

Library of Congress Cataloging-in-Publication Data

Names: Kenan, Tessa, author.
Title: Hooray for firefighters! / by Tessa Kenan.
Description: Minneapolis : Lerner Publications, 2017. | Series: Bumba books. Hooray for community helpers! | Audience: Age 4–7. | Audience: K to Grade 3. | Includes bibliographical references and index.
Identifiers: LCCN 2016044351 (print) | LCCN 2016046905 (ebook) | ISBN 9781512433494 (library bound : alk. paper) | ISBN 9781512455519 (paperback : alk. paper) | ISBN 9781512450330 (eb pdf)
Subjects: LCSH: Fire extinction—Juvenile literature. | Fire fighters—Juvenile literature.
Classification: LCC TH9148 .K455 2017 (print) | LCC TH9148 (ebook) | DDC 363.37—dc23

LC record available at https://lccn.loc.gov/2016044351

Manufactured in the United States of America
1 — CG — 7/15/17

Expand learning beyond the printed book. Download free, complementary educational resources for this book from our website, www.lernerresource.com.

Table of Contents

Firefighters Keep Us Safe

Firefighters work in our communities.

They help keep us safe from fires.

Firefighters put out fires.

They act fast!

They slide down a pole.

Each firefighter wears a suit, a helmet, and gloves.

The uniform keeps them safe from fires.

How might uniforms keep firefighters safe?

Firefighters ride in a fire truck

to the fire.

Loud sirens sound.

Lights flash.

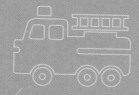

Firefighters work quickly.

They use a hose to spray

water on the fire.

Why must firefighters work quickly?

Some fires are in tall buildings.

Firefighters climb a ladder.

This firefighter goes into the

burning building.

She looks for people trapped inside.

Firefighters teach us about

fire safety too.

Escape plans are important.

What else might firefighters teach us?

Firefighters have a big job.

They work hard to keep us safe.

Firefighter Tools

ladder

fire truck

helmet

suit

axe

gloves

hose

Picture Glossary

burning

being on fire

communities

groups of people who live in the same area

sirens

devices that make loud sounds

uniform

a special set of clothes worn for work

23

Read More

Bellisario, Gina. *Let's Meet a Firefighter.* Minneapolis: Millbrook Press, 2013.

Parkes, Elle. *Hooray for Police Officers!* Minneapolis: Lerner Publications, 2017.

Riggs, Kate. *Fire Trucks.* Mankato, MN: Creative Education, 2015.

Index

Photo Credits